Big or Little?

Adria F. Klein

Dominie Press, Inc.

Publisher: Christine Yuen
Series Editors: Adria F. Klein & Alan Trussell-Cullen
Editors: Bob Rowland & Paige Sanderson
Designers: Gary Hamada & Lois Stanfield
Photographers: SportsPhoto (Page 4 – elephant); Graham Meadows
(Page 4 – mouse); Lois Stanfield, LightSource Images (pages 5-10).

Published by:

🔱 **Dominie Press, Inc.**

1949 Kellogg Avenue
Carlsbad, California 92008 USA

www.dominie.com

ISBN 0-7685-1507-6

Printed in Singapore by PH Productions Pte Ltd

1 2 3 4 5 6 PH 03 02 01

ITP

Table of Contents

What is big?
What is little?

Flowers on a plant can be big.
Flowers on a plant can be little.

Are the flowers on this plant big or little?

A car can be big.
A car can be little.

Is this car big or little?

People can be big.

People can be little.

Am I big?

Am I little?

I am in the middle!

Picture Glossary

car:

people:

flower:

Index